Other books by C. Leslie Charles:

Bless Your Stress (Yes! Press)
It Means You're Still Alive!

All Is Not Lost (Yes! Press)
The Healing Journey Through Crisis, Grief and Loss

Why Is Everyone So Cranky? (Hyperion)
The Ten Trends Complicating Our Lives and What We Can Do About Them

The Instant Trainer (McGraw-Hill)
Quick Tips on How to Teach Others What You Know

Rule #One (Successories)
If You Don't Take Care Of The Customer, Someone Else Will

The Customer Service Companion (Yes! Press)
The Essential Handbook For Those Who Serve Others

The Companion Study Guide (Yes! Press)
A Self-Directed Customer Service Seminar

www.LeslieCharles.com

Especially for:

Here's to the power
of positive persistence!

[signature]

What readers say about STICK TO IT!

Every morning I flip open a page and that's my thought for the day—I don't know what I would do without your book. I cannot begin to thank you enough.
—Judy Kendall, Wife, Mother, Special Ed Administrative Secretary

I love your book! It's a great source for motivation and keeping things in perspective for me and members of my fitness classes.
—Terry Ferebee, Medical Center Wellness Director

I've enjoyed your STICK TO IT! messages and want to let you know we are holding my father's "Alive and Well!" party this weekend. Thanks for the idea!
—Tim Kosier, Director of Services for People With Developmental Disabilities

We use STICK TO IT! for our monthly staff meetings. Reading a few of the essays and quotations sets an optimistic tone. I couldn't think of a better way to begin.
—Evie Bishop, Medical Practice Manager

Yes! Press
East Lansing, MI

The Power of Positive Persistence

C. Leslie Charles

Printed in the United States of America

Published by:

Yes! Press

PO Box 956
East Lansing, MI 48826
517-675-7535

Cover and Book Design by Diana L.Grinwis
Cover Portrait by Allison Eastin

Publisher's Cataloging in Publication Data

Charles, C. Leslie.
    Stick To It! : the power of positive persistence / C. Leslie
Charles. -- [New ed.].
    p. cm.
    ISBN 0-9644621-0-9

    1. Success. 2. Conduct of life. I. Title
BJ1611.C43 1995, 2002   158'.1
                                     QBI95-20199
    Library of Congress Catalog Card Number   95-60861

ISBN 0-9644621-0-9

Table of Contents

Persistence

What is persistence?
It is the cornerstone of achievement.
Persistence is an essential skill
that blends self-encouragement and commitment.

Persistence is the choice to keep on going,
the willingness to try one more time.
It is a personal commitment to stand your ground
and prevail in the face of adversity.

Persistence is creativity and flexibility.
It helps us discover new ways
when our old ways no longer work.
It is the decision to create new directions
when old ones no longer hold promise.

Persistence is the self-belief, confidence, and action
that helps us stick to it. Persistence is a way of life.

—C. Leslie Charles

Dedication

To my children, Ron, Cathy, and Rob, for their hilarious stories of all the things they got away with when they were small, despite my watchful eye. To my mom and dad, Julie and Bob, for telling me I could do anything I wanted once I set my mind to it. To my life partner, Random, for his twenty years of loving companionship, disarming wit, behind the scenes endless hard work, and merciless editing. And to my friends, clients, and audiences who consider my ideas worthy.

Foreword...

This book, like any truthful writing about personal experience, is one gear in the "works" of that mechanism we label self-development. Like all gears, and most human beings, it works best in the company of others with similar goals.

Growing, learning, and risking are some of the behaviors that separate people who are truly alive from those who are just marking time.

In our lifelong pursuits we are continually fighting old habits, experiences, and attitudes that encourage us to remain creatures of habit; inflexible and unyielding.

So one book, even a very good one such as this, will not move you far from your foundation, unless you really want it to. Yet, one book, or even one pivotal phrase, can, and has been, the start of many amazing journeys of change.

One book leads to others, then to tapes and seminars, and back to books again until we have constructed a new foundation for being. One based on thoughtfulness, reason, and caring.

The cornerstone of this book is the understanding that we are all able to improve through *gradualism:* the consistent and persistent application of new and better ideas; new ways of thinking.

How you think defines who you are. And despite your past, good or bad, you *do* have control over your thoughts. You choose, every minute of every day, the kind of person you want to be; the kind of life you want to live.

Since I have known Leslie Charles for eighteen years, I'll share with you a little known story that perfectly mirrors what gradualism is all about.

When I first met Leslie in 1975 she was just kicking in the afterburners on her own quest for personal growth. She was in the middle of a major career upgrade, raising teenage kids, and going back to school yet again. She was also trying, for the first time in her life, to get in decent physical shape.

I remember going along on her first jog. She could only shuffle a quarter mile. Trying to stretch, her fingers could hardly reach her knees: a seemingly hopeless situation from my perspective, but Leslie saw only opportunity.

After several years, many hours of stretching and a reasonable exercise program, Leslie could put her hands on the floor. For a time she competed in 10K races and she has arms and legs that look like those of a seasoned athlete. She's not compulsive about working out (or personal growth), she is simply consistent and persistent!

Gradualism is perhaps the most difficult concept for human beings to grasp. Leslie wrote the book, this book, to offer her insights on this tough issue. So let this volume and this author be one of the gears in your life's self-development works. Use them as a springboard for your own greater explorations, or as a touchstone for renewal.

Personal understanding is like a prism; a slight shift of angle and a whole new world is illuminated. New information begins to make sense and old ideas acquire even deeper meaning. Life is a great adventure and it's nice to have a few good books along the way. This is one of them.

Robert Carr

Author's Notes

This is a thoughtful book, and a special one. What makes it special is you, the reader, and how you will choose to apply these ideas. Whether you bought this for yourself, or received it as a gift, you will decide how best to approach each reading.

You are probably a busy person with many demands on your time, but this book is designed with that in mind. Each essay or quotation is just a small, single thought, yet they do hold the promise of something larger; that all depends on you.

I have attempted to present my ideas in a light and simple manner, but you will find worthy lessons if you take the time to look for them.

While this is original material, many of these thoughts will seem familiar. No doubt, you've thought about these concepts before, and faced similar experiences, but perhaps my approach will offer a new perspective.

You know as well as I, that a thoughtful and consciously considered life is richer, fuller, and inherently more satisfying than an unconsidered one.

Each item in this book represents a small, separate dimension of life; intricate components that make up the whole of existence. Each is worth examining in depth.

I hope you will read, reread, reflect upon, and revisit the ideas that touch your heart. My hope is that this book gives you numerous ideas and insights to explore, expand upon, and apply in your life.

I also hope the message, STICK TO IT! will encourage you to persist as you live, learn, grow, and face new adventures and challenges. Read and enjoy!

STICK TO IT!

It all began with the silver sticker; a simple tool conceived to help my audiences remember key ideas covered in seminars, speeches, and training programs.

People loved them and over the years I have given away thousands of these little reminders. They wind up on computers, desks, dashboards, bathroom mirrors, refrigerator doors, and workout room walls. One was even used in a pinch to hold up a torn skirt hem.

A **STICK TO IT!** sticker is perfect wherever you need a little inspiration. When the going gets rough and chocolate seems the only comfort in the world, a well-placed sticker will help remind you of the goals you have set and the long term rewards of sticking to them.

If you would like a few original silver foil **STICK TO IT!** stickers for your very own, just send me a stamped, self-addressed envelope at **Yes! Press** and I will make sure you receive them.

*A crisis is simply an opportunity
for you to practice
what you preach.*

— *C. Leslie Charles*

It All Begins With Attitude

Much has been written about the importance of attitude, and most of us realize that our attitude affects the kinds of decisions we make and the actions we take. Some people tend to see the positive side of a situation while others view the negative.

How about you? How has your attitude affected the kinds of decisions you've made in your life, and the relationships you've established and maintained? I am convinced that life is 80% attitude and 20% technique; if your attitude is in the right place, you'll make the right decisions. If you have a positive attitude, the right words will come out of your mouth.

We all know that, basically, we get out of life what we expect and, of course, our attitude influences our expectations. What expectations do you have about yourself and your world? What attitude adjustments might you need to make in order to improve your outlook?

If you want to be more positive, start using positive words rather than negative ones. Smile more. Make it a habit to compliment others rather than criticize. And look on the optimistic side of a situation.

Develop an *attitude of gratitude*. Celebrate what you have, and help others look on the bright side as well. You know that what you give out will come back to you. Attitude: it's the perfect place to begin!

*You can wait forever
for the right moment
or you can make this moment
the right one.*

— *C. Leslie Charles*

Are You Ready Yet?

Some of us seem to spend life in a perpetual state of "getting ready" rather than actually accomplishing anything. What prevents us from taking those first, critical steps and why do we fail to follow through?

We might feel overwhelmed and think that the first step has to be a huge one, or that it must be perfect. Or we may be surrounded by negative people, and doubt our ability to achieve a major goal. It's possible we think we are unworthy of such an accomplishment. But even if we see our goal or dream as a long shot, we will never really know until we try.

That first step is the critical one, regardless of its size. Several years ago I created my quarterly newsletter, *The Charles Report,* as a small step toward convincing myself that I could indeed, one day be an author. It's taken me awhile, but even as STICK TO IT! goes to press, I have another volume waiting in the wings.

If you're stuck in "getting ready" let yourself take that first small step, even if doesn't seem like the perfect one or the most logical. Just do something. Get started.

Chances are, wherever you begin is correct for you. Trust that first step. Regardless of its size, it is the *right one* for you. First do it, then stick to it. That's how getting ready turns into getting things done!

The next time you feel
as if you're walking a tightrope,
check to see if it's lying on the ground.

— *C. Leslie Charles*

It's Up To You...

In virtually every situation that presents itself, many options exist. And while life is filled with choices, we make so many of them at an unconscious level that only the big ones tend to show. How aware are you of the choices you make? I've learned that I can consciously choose how I think, feel, or act. And so can you.

Whether an event is unfortunate or exciting, happy or sad, elected or imposed, the outcome depends on you. The process of making choices can be effortless, complicated, simple, or difficult. It can be conscious or automatic. But in each experience, you have a choice as to how you will respond. It may take awhile before you choose; you may first need to heal your wounds or process the experience. But it is *you* who decides whether what you're facing is an obstacle or an opportunity; a crisis or a challenge. It's all in how you choose to look at it.

You can choose to be intimidated or inspired, confident or insecure. When it comes to emotions such as anger, depression, resentment, or fear, you can choose to remain in that state of mind, or you can consciously change. Ultimately, behavior is a choice.

Once you begin making more conscious choices in your life, it will become a pattern you'll stick to; how could you possibly want to choose anything else?

If we looked at the world through a child's eyes, each day we'd find a new surprise.

— *C. Leslie Charles*

Cause For Celebration

Birthdays, holidays, anniversaries, and major accomplishments are occasions formally earmarked for celebration. Yet every single day there are things worth celebrating. Just waking up is a good place to start!

Everyday experiences such as good health, hard work, loved ones, cherished sights, smells, sounds, tastes, and even textures that are pleasurable to touch can be great sources of appreciation—if we notice them!

But we often take these little things for granted. What a difference it might make if we occasionally took a few moments to reflect on the positives in life, celebrated them, and made them special; had a party for no reason at all, as a child might.

What's worth celebrating in your life and how long has it been since you celebrated a *personal* special occasion? Why wait for the calendar to tell you when it's time to have fun? If you can't think of anything big, then look for something small. Maybe today you can get into the spirit and begin celebrating the little things in your life that make a big difference.

This is just a small reminder that it's your life, and *your* personal timetable. Celebrating is something you can do anytime, anywhere, with anyone, and for absolutely any reason at all. Now, that's something to celebrate in itself!

When we act out of fear we often create the very outcome we're trying to avoid.

— *C. Leslie Charles*

Fear: It's Nothing To Be Afraid Of

We all have things we're afraid of. Fear is a common and basic emotion. We may fear rejection, embarrassment, abandonment, failure, and maybe even success. Yes, there will always be things we fear, but to what extent will we let it influence us?

You can let fear control you, or you can control your fear and take action anyway. This distinction is important because fear can literally immobilize us. We might use it as an excuse to give up, or worse, to not even try.

When I started college, after having dropped out of high school not once but twice, I was terrified. I had no idea if I could succeed and dreaded the possibility of failing one more time.

Just walking onto the campus was intimidating, and part of me wanted to run away. But I attended class every day, studied hard in spite of my fears, and graduated with honors.

I learned that achieving something new requires stretching your capabilities; that one can only build self-confidence by first laying it on the line. To experience success, you must first place yourself in a situation where failure is one of the possibilities.

It feels great knowing you faced your fears squarely and took action in spite of how you felt. You've done this before, and you can do it again. Keep reminding yourself that every time you risk failure, you are also risking success!

*Focus is the ability
to get outside of yourself
and fix on your goal
rather than your fears.*

— *C. Leslie Charles*

Adjusting Your Focus

People who set and achieve their goals are masters at focusing. They create an image of what they want, devise a plan for moving toward their desired outcome, and focus on the steps it takes to make it happen. It's been said that obstacles are what we see when we take our eyes off our goal, and it takes a lot of belief and focus to stay the course.

When a horse and rider approach a high fence, neither of them can see over it. The rider focuses not on the fence, but *beyond* it. When the rider concentrates on a vision of what lies on the other side of the fence, rather than the fence itself, the jump is cleared. If the rider focuses on the fence, the horse often hesitates, stops dead, or hits the rail on the way over. The rider makes the fence a *barrier* by focusing on it.

When you have a goal, you need to fix it in your mind and project your vision. If you get scared or plagued with self-doubt, refocus on your vision of the desired outcome, not your fears. This will prevent your fears from becoming a barrier. By focusing on the vision of what you want, you'll actually begin to set up the kinds of circumstances (action steps) that will help you achieve it.

Focusing is a powerful tool; just be sure to concentrate on the outcomes you *want* rather than what you don't want. Your ability to stay focused can help make your vision a reality.

When in doubt, lighten up.
It may not change the situation,
but it has the potential of changing you.

— *C. Leslie Charles*

Humor Works

While life is serious business, we could all learn to take ourselves less seriously. If you walk through life with a lighter step and continually look for humor in everyday situations, you'll have a better chance of overcoming hardships.

If you're able to smile instead of scream, or chuckle instead of criticize, you'll stay healthier and happier. If you can shrug things off rather than get stressed out, or relax instead of retaliate, you'll be better able to work and live harmoniously with others.

A quick smile can dissolve conflict, relax tension, and ease an otherwise stressful situation. A hearty laugh can break the ice, lend perspective, and neutralize an otherwise intimidating event. Humor can be a bridge between strangers, and a welcome relief when tempers start to flare. It's a great way to maintain your perspective.

Of course, the best source for humor is yourself; you'll *never* run out of material! To keep on keeping on, just remind yourself to lighten up. You'll be less tense and more flexible.

So, the next time things begin to fall apart, just stand back and smile instead of getting in the middle of the fray. Everyone else will think that you must know something they don't. And they'll be right!

Failure only exists as long as you let it.
Rather than fearing failure,
be afraid of not trying.

— *C. Leslie Charles*

The Rewards Of Risk Taking

Many people live their lives driven by fear rather than choice. They avoid rather than pursue, opt for security rather than adventure, and often make decisions based on apprehension rather than desire. Living a full life requires taking risks, yet some people do everything possible to avoid them.

What does risk mean? It means change. Risking is letting go of that which is known, predictable, safe, and secure. It means stepping into the unknown, and entering a situation that holds many possibilities. Risking means planning, calculating, and predicting what might happen with little certainty; trusting one's ability to create a positive outcome.

To risk without planning can be a foolish act. But risk with foresight, desire, and consideration can be an adventure! Of course, not all risks work out. But most risk takers declare they would rather risk and fail than never take a chance, and I agree.

The possible rewards of risk taking include growth, insight, confidence, experience, education, and success. The results of avoiding risk are often lost confidence or regret.

If there's something you'd like to do, but you've been holding back, consider taking that first step. It's usually the hardest, and just the act of venturing forth can be a reward in itself!

*If we're willing to take the blame
for our mistakes,
we also need to give ourselves credit
when we do something right.*

— *C. Leslie Charles*

There's A Better Choice Than Insecurity

We all have our insecurities. A handsome, successful friend of mine admitted that despite his money, silk suits, and good looks, what he first saw when he looked in the mirror was his thinning hair. I was shocked to realize he was more affected by his insecurities than his assets.

We could all feel much better about ourselves if we were to replace our feelings of inferiority with visions of capability or competence. It's no surprise that focusing on self-doubt erodes our confidence, yet we do it.

When my self-esteem was at its lowest, I allowed my insecurities to dominate. It was common for me to feel so self-conscious and inferior that I avoided people or situations that challenged me. And sadly, I was threatened by the very individuals I wanted to emulate. You've probably figured out that our biggest hurdles are often internal: self-imposed limitations, fears, and insecurities.

How can you overcome them? Persistently remind yourself of your skills and abilities. Emphasize what you *can* do rather than what you can't. Choose to focus on what you do right rather than wrong. Encourage yourself; give yourself credit when you do something especially well, and most of all, just enjoy being who you are.

And the best part? When you make the choice of feeling good about yourself, you'll attract others who feel good about themselves, too.

Your mind is the key through which you unlock all your potential.

— *C. Leslie Charles*

It's All In Your Mind

You may already know that you talk to yourself and conduct lengthy internal dialogues about virtually everything that happens to you. Without saying a word aloud, you continually interpret events. You judge, appraise, compliment, or criticize yourself and others every day. It's called *self-talk*.

Is your self-talk constructive or destructive? Start listening to what you say to yourself. This is important because it is your thoughts that create your reality. If you think things are awful, horrible, and you just can't handle it, you will feel like a *victim* of circumstances.

If, on the other hand, you view a situation as admittedly difficult but, with effort, ultimately doable, you encourage yourself to be a *victor*. Put simply, how you talk to yourself is entirely up to you. You can create healthy, encouraging self-talk or you can make yourself miserable; it's your call.

For it is not what actually happens to you, it's how you define it internally that counts. If you realize you are engaging in negative, defeatist self-talk, replace it with positive, hopeful dialogue. If you find yourself feeling inadequate or incapable, tell yourself that you can do it. Because you *can*.

Even if your life does become temporarily disrupted, positive self-talk can help you put it all back together again. It's all there; in your mind.

Keep the chips off your shoulder
and in your hand
so you have control over where they fall.

— *C. Leslie Charles*

So Much To Learn, So Little Time...

Are you an active learner, a seeker of self-knowledge? While learning is infinitely rewarding, it can also be difficult. Some people reject or avoid moments of insight while others are open and receptive, despite the discomfort it may bring. How about you?

Every experience, especially painful ones, can bring you knowledge and opportunities if you're willing to figure out what the lesson is. Mind you, I'm not suggesting this is easy!

Some of life's lessons are harsh, challenging, and uncomfortable. They may require intense soul searching or admissions we'd rather avoid. Sometimes we may need to take a leap of faith and trust the learning process, knowing there will be rewards down the road. This is hard.

When facing a tough experience, look for the lesson. Be willing to ask yourself what there is to be learned or gained. It might take awhile to figure it out if you have some healing to do first, or need extra time to work through your resistance.

Be patient and persistent. It's amazing how much you can learn, gain, and grow when you are open minded enough to treat your experiences as a learning ground. Your life will be fuller, richer, and more peaceful.

Maybe you could ask yourself right now what lesson is waiting in the wings. Is it time for you to learn a little more?

*Self-doubt can simply be an indicator
that you're on unfamiliar ground.
Use it as a beacon
rather than a barrier
so you can keep on going.*

—*C. Leslie Charles*

Persistence Pays Off!

Study the lives of achievers and you will find one common trait among them. It's not intelligence, money, status, or power. It's persistence!

If there is something you want to achieve, the one quality that can successfully propel you toward your goal is your ability to stick to it. That's what you can have in common with some of the greatest achievers of all time; the ability to persist!

Looking back on my life, persistence is the one quality that helped me slowly and systematically transform from a high school dropout to college graduate and entrepreneur.

If you are wondering how you can become more persistent, here are some suggestions. When you get discouraged, look outward for inspiration or encouragement so you can take another step: talk to a friend, read a book, or find an inspiring quotation.

When you get hurt, give yourself time to heal, and then move on. When you fall down, be willing to pull yourself back up. And when you fail, write it off as *experience* rather than failure. Your ability to stick to it will help you advance; step by step, day by day.

Why keep on going? Because the next time you try may be the one big breakthrough you're looking for; that last effort may be it. So when you feel as if you're ready to give up, remind yourself that sticking to it can make all the difference in the world.

*Don't send me flowers when I die—
give them to me now
so we can appreciate their beauty
together!*

—*C. Leslie Charles*

Alive And Well!

In 1990 I had the joy of hosting my parents' 50th wedding anniversary party. It was truly a delight celebrating with family, friends, and acquaintances I hadn't seen in years.

Gatherings such as this are generally restricted to weddings and funerals, and once the younger generation is all settled down, there are regrettably few reasons for everyone to congregate. It struck me that I might not see many of these people again until someone in our family or circle of friends died, and that bothered me. Perhaps it would even be *my* funeral! Imagine, all of these wonderful people coming to pay their respects, and I would miss it!

Then it occurred to me: what if you could somehow gather together all of the people who would care enough about you to attend your funeral, only do it *before* you die? An *Alive and Well!* party. The invitation could read: "If you consider yourself enough of a friend of mine so that if I died today you would attend my funeral, please come to my *Alive and Well!* party instead. This way, together, we can celebrate my *life* rather than honor my death."

Attendance at the party would exempt them from having to attend my funeral. I plan on having my *Alive and Well!* party soon. Be sure to let me know when you have yours!

The harder you try
to avoid the lessons you need to learn,
the more persistently they will pursue you.

— *C. Leslie Charles*

The Honest Truth

I once heard a therapist speak on mental health. Before her fifteen minute presentation, I found myself wondering how she could possibly offer any practical advice in such a short time frame. But she did.

The gist of her speech was, "Be honest about what you see and hear, what you say to yourself and others, and be honest about what you do." Through the years I've remembered her words and tried to incorporate them into my life. Her simple message encouraged self-responsibility and ownership: that we admit to what's *really* going on in our life.

Honesty necessitates that we square things with ourself before we confront someone else. It can help us control our defensiveness and minimize our tendency to blame others. By being honest with ourself we can better identify how we may have contributed to a situation. We can claim ownership for our part in a conflict or misunderstanding, or admit when we are wrong. It can also serve as a reminder that the one person to whom we are always accountable is our own self.

Are you being honest about what's going on in your life? Are you contributing in an honest way to your relationships? It's infinitely simple in concept, and ultimately hard in application. Isn't that the honest truth!

*How you behave
is a statement about your character;
how I respond to your behavior
is a statement about mine.*

— *C. Leslie Charles*

A Different Look At Differences

Opposites attract, but while we may initially be drawn to someone who's quite different than we are, after awhile, those refreshing differences can become wearing. Over time, we might try to convince those who are so different from us that they should become more *like* us.

Many marriages and life partnerships dissolve because both parties are unable to reconcile their differences, yet those same differences initially made the relationship work. What happens?

For one thing, we may perceive another person's differing attitude as resistance or obstinacy rather than being honestly different. Or we may consider a different viewpoint as opposition rather than simply another opinion. The best way to reconcile these differences is to communicate; to discuss issues in depth and explore without judgment, to discover the intent and feelings behind one's words or behaviors. We may find that we have more in common than we think.

Of course, this requires give and take, suspension of judgment, and openness to different ideas and divergent perspectives. Most of us get so entrenched in our own viewpoint we have no room for differing opinions. But when we are willing to view things from the other side, we often discover we are not really so different after all!

Success always begins with a thought but it is achieved through action.

— *C. Leslie Charles*

It's Almost As If...

You have far more potential than you think and maybe it's time you realized it. What do you want for yourself? How close are you to what you want, and how will you get from here to there?

Motivational writers encourage us to apply the power of our mind; to think *as if* we are already the person we want to become, to see ourself as successful and accomplished.

Do you want to feel more confident? Then start behaving *as if* you are a confident person; do the things confident people do. Would you like to be more positive? Then think positive thoughts; smile more often, compliment others, and look on the bright side.

By behaving *as if*, you discover how truly capable you are. You learn you can do more than you thought; that you have far more potential than you might have believed.

This process may sound silly but it works. I wouldn't be where I am without it. Are you ready to begin?

Identify something you want to do. Then pretend (yes, pretend) as if you can do it; as if you are *already* the person you want to become. Begin doing the things this individual would do. You'll find you are far more capable than you thought; it's *as if* the person you wanted to be was right there inside you all the time—and it is!

*The acknowledgment
that you're feeling down
can be the first step
toward looking up again.*

—*C. Leslie Charles*

The Up Side Of Being Down

With so many "be positive" messages in this book, it may be well to consider the other side, too. Chronic bad moods, crankiness, depression, and feelings of alienation, confusion, or frustration need to be dealt with, not avoided. They are messages that we have some unfinished business with a person, event, or issue.

Our feelings may relate to something from our past or present. They can be a concern or worry about the future. Regardless of their origin, we need to check out these feelings.

In fact, any ongoing situation that provokes strong emotions or conflict needs to be explored, confronted, or brought to some level of closure, even if acceptance is the only option.

Life can be joyful, and it can also be very, very difficult. You need to stay honest with yourself so you can acknowledge and work through your tough times rather than avoid them. Denial can seem like a seductive option, but it leads to more problems. So does procrastination.

Your emotions can be a signal that something is wrong. Listen to them, and take appropriate action so you can get on with your life. And the up side of this approach? The positive thinking skills you build today can help you get through the challenges or down times you will face in the future.

*The best time to celebrate is
the here and now;
what a great present to give yourself!*

— *C. Leslie Charles*

Give Yourself A Present

Where do you spend your time? No, I'm not asking *where* you are, but *when*. Some people spend a lot of time thinking about the past, longing for the good old days. Others are fixed on the future, waiting, hoping for what tomorrow may bring, or worrying about what might happen. It seems as if we're everywhere but where we are!

While we all have a past, and while we need to plan for our future, the only time frame over which we have any kind of control is the present; the here and now. So many people waste their present moments because their minds are focused either backward or forward. I hope you're not one of them.

What you do each day influences your future and there are many advantages to living in the here and now. For example, you can let go of old, painful memories or regrets that may have haunted you. You can lay worry aside, and fully live one day at a time. You can spend your time planning or taking an action step rather than worrying it away.

By living in the present you can make daily decisions and take the steps that move you toward the future you want. Indeed, living in the here and now is the best kind of "present" you can possibly give yourself!

People's negative behaviors say more about them than they do about you.

— *C. Leslie Charles*

The Bane Of Blame

We've all experienced disappointment, crisis, and tragedy. We've been hurt, mistreated, taken advantage of, or rejected. We all have a history, and it can be tempting to blame our past for ruining our present. But blame keeps a bad memory alive, no matter how long ago it happened, and it can grow in intensity over time. We may not realize that getting caught up in blaming renders us incapable of forgetting, forgiving, and forging on.

So why do we do it, you may ask. Blame is a defense mechanism that shields us against hurt, anger, and disappointment. It can also be a convenient cop out or a means by which we justify retaliation. Blame can be an excuse for inaction, or resistance to taking responsibility.

While we cannot magically eradicate our past, we *can* come to terms with it. And we can choose how we want to handle unfortunate events from now on.

I learned through experience that once I gave up blaming others, I had a stronger sense of responsibility and more control over what happened to me. I had more choices.

If you're hanging onto any kind of blame, let it go, because the only person you're punishing is yourself. You can gain a lot by giving up something that gives you absolutely nothing back—blame!

The effort it takes
to create a good excuse
can always be put to better use.

—*C. Leslie Charles*

Excuse Me!

Life can be rich with excuses. One leads to another, and before long, we have sacrificed weeks, months, or maybe even precious years making excuses for all the things we think we cannot do, should not do, or want to do, but are afraid to do. Our potential is too important to waste, yet we squander our talent and creativity inventing and justifying excuses.

Perhaps we could instead *harness* that energy and use it for goal setting, brainstorming, problem solving, and action steps. Nice idea, so why don't we do it?

One handy excuse is that the timing or circumstances are wrong. Yet, they may never improve. We could go on making excuses forever.

But excuses don't get us anywhere.

Admittedly, there may be a time when waiting for the right moment *is* the best thing to do, but we must acknowledge whether we're truly waiting or procrastinating. We need to know that it's not just another excuse.

Spend some time thinking about what you want in your life, and what you're doing to make it happen. If you come up with a large gap between the two, you might want to ask yourself what excuses you've been making and how valid they are.

This exercise may just give you the inspiration you've been looking for so you can begin taking that first step instead of making yet one more excuse.

Trying to take the easy way out can make for hard times.

— C. Leslie Charles

Dealing With The Difficult

Life can be difficult. Although I try to focus on joy and happiness in my life, I've faced some very painful and trying times. Recently, I gained some insights about this subject. We could describe two major types of difficult experiences in life; ones that are positive, and ones that are painful.

The *positive difficult* times are periods of challenge and adventure; when we can't wait to get out of bed and face the day. We summon our inner resources and plunge forward, eager to meet the charge.

And then there are the *painful difficult* times when we are hurt, disappointed, or immersed in self-doubt. It may be tempting to give up because we hurt so much, and it's hard to identify our options.

Yet, in both our positive *and* our painful times, we use the same set of skills and resources to prevail. What makes things feel so different is our *perception* of each situation!

So the next time you're facing a painful or difficult situation, remind yourself that you have what it takes to prevail. You have the persistence, strength, imagination, and desire to survive deep inside you.

Just knowing how many times you have already successfully faced *painful difficult* times might help make your next difficult experience just a little less so. You can summon up that inner power and let it help you persist.

The state of each of your relationships is a statement about you.

— *C. Leslie Charles*

A Toxic Topic

Relationships can be wonderful or wearisome, affirming or anxiety provoking. Some relationships, such as the family we're born into, are fixed; others, such as friends or lovers, are elected. Some relationships support and nurture us; some don't. And ironically, some of our closest relationships aren't all that good for us.

As you evaluate your relationships, here's a question to consider. Do you have any *toxic* people in your life: ones who intimidate, manipulate, browbeat, excessively criticize, demean, guilt trip, or try to control you?

Toxic people foster dysfunctional relationships; they are takers, not givers. They feed off insecurities and emotional indebtedness, and assume positions of superiority. You know you are involved in a toxic relationship by the instant tension, defensiveness, discomfort, feelings of inferiority, or buried rage you experience when in the person's company.

While the ideal solution would be to somehow magically transform or completely avoid a toxic individual, this might not be possible. If complete absence is not an option, you might consider how to best manage toxic relationships for the least possible damage to you.

If you have any toxic people in your life, consider how you can minimize your exposure to them, or at least reduce their influence. Toxic people are best taken in small doses.

There's a difference between resistance and readiness.

— *C. Leslie Charles*

What's Your State Of Readiness?

You know the frustration of trying to help someone who is unreceptive. No matter how hard you try, the other party just isn't ready to listen. This happens to all of us. Our *state of readiness* depends on our attitude at any given moment.

Take this book, for example. It's possible you are reading these ideas at a time when you are completely receptive and open to all kinds of possibilities. If so, you are in a peak state of readiness. On the other hand, you may be in a frame of mind where these ideas have little effect on you.

A lot depends on what's happening in your life at this moment and where your mental energy is. If you're in a turmoil and your defense mechanisms are helping you hold it all together, or if your self-esteem is low, then you might attempt to "protect" yourself from ideas that seem threatening.

That's why it can be a good idea to reread this book at a later time. Perhaps you could share or discuss it with a friend. Some of what you read may be exciting, some of it may make little sense, and some of these ideas might initially threaten or challenge you.

But don't give up; just read, consider, and apply what fits for you right now, then go back for more when you're ready. Depending on your state of readiness, you'll get whatever you're looking for, every time.

*The next time someone
pushes your buttons
remind yourself
that you're the one who installed them.*

— *C. Leslie Charles*

Return To Sender

The medical community acknowledges the relationship between our psychology and physiology; our brain and body are connected. Understanding this brain-body connection can save you unnecessary stress and tension.

For example, some people live in a state of anxiety, resentment, and anger for years, over a situation long since passed, and this extended inner turmoil can take a toll on their health. Don't let it happen to you!

If there is an incident you've been playing, replaying, and keeping alive in your thoughts, let it go. Accept that you cannot punish others through your negative thoughts, no matter how strong or consistent they are.

If indeed, the brain and body are connected, consider what happens every time you "zap" someone with your anger, hatred, or resentment. Whatever you send out to someone else cycles through your entire being—from your brain through your body—and *you* become the unfortunate recipient of all your negative emotions. The only person you end up zapping is yourself!

Maybe it's time to revise your strategy and only send out to others whatever is fit for you: peace, enlightenment, tolerance, or love.

*Life begins to get a little easier
when you're willing
to make hard choices.*

— *C. Leslie Charles*

The "Me" In You

There are two parts of you, and you can determine which influences you most by answering this question: do you live your life as who you *want* to be, or who you think you *should* be?

One part of you, Me^1, is the true you; the intuitive, honest, unaffected, knowledgeable, ethical, capable self. Me^2 is the part of you that has been trained, indoctrinated, influenced, and shaped by external factors and other people's expectations.

Me^2 is filled with self-imposed judgments, excuses, fears, insecurities, defense mechanisms, and obligations. Its dialogue is replete with guilt-laden words such as, *should, must, ought to, have to*; words which distance you from your true self.

Me^2 tends to be harsh, self-critical and more vocal than Me^1 and just by its description, you probably recognize how Me^2 undermines your self-esteem.

The Me^1 part of you is intrinsically honest, principled, accepting, open, and willing to learn. It will guide you toward valid, healthy options if you're willing to take the risk. Me^1 choices can be difficult in the short term (challenging) but beneficial in the long term (offering growth). Me^2 choices are just the opposite, fostering denial, avoidance, and excuses.

What's the point? Listen carefully to yourself and determine who's in charge, Me^1 or Me^2. The choice is yours; who would you rather be?

The minute you dig in your heels you've just lost ground.

— *C. Leslie Charles*

Hear Me Out

A good definition of conflict is a *duelogue*; that is, both parties are speaking and no one is listening. When you find yourself in a conflict, a good rule of thumb is to be the first person to listen; you'll have no competition, that's for sure.

We've all heard the saying "what goes around comes around" and it certainly applies to listening. You'll get further if you make a concerted attempt to identify what the situation means to the other party. Trying to listen from the other person's perspective will help you avoid the "right-wrong trap," making it easier for all concerned to work toward a mutually acceptable solution.

You might also learn something about why other people behave as they do if you're willing to keep your mouth closed and your mind open. In other words, listen more, judge less. Ask rather than tell.

If you are first willing to listen, chances are, by the time you get around to speaking, the other party will be more receptive to what you have to say. When listening, stay focused on the speaker and avoid mentally arguing with what is being said. Do your best to identify and relate.

When you do speak, avoid sounding defensive. In short, if you take the time to listen to others, they will be more likely to listen to you.

Every time we blame,
we give up our ability
to affect, influence, or change a situation.

— *C. Leslie Charles*

A Second Chance

It's tempting to blame others when a conflict or misunderstanding occurs, but the satisfaction derived from blame is only temporary. If you're looking for a constructive, long-term solution, here is a suggestion that can have far reaching effects.

According to Sidney Simon, in each of our relationships, we help create, contribute to, and cooperate in whatever exists between ourself and the other party. He suggests that relationships don't just happen, nor do they just go wrong; both parties share some responsibility for the outcome.

In each of your relationships, especially the troublesome ones, you can at any time change the dynamics between yourself and the other person.

How? By changing your behavior! When *you* make a change, the relationship changes.

Ask yourself, "How have I helped create, contribute to, or cooperate in the dynamics of this relationship?" Determine which of your behaviors work and which don't. Then ask, "What do I need to do differently?" And try a new approach without considering who is right or wrong.

Blame may be convenient, and perhaps initially satisfying, but it won't change or improve anything for the long term. This approach gives you a chance—for a second chance!

State of mind
affects state of body
and state of body
affects state of mind.

— *C. Leslie Charles*

Try This For A Change

If you've ever been depressed, you probably have a clear memory of what the body language of depression looks and feels like. When we are depressed our body appears to be on terminal droop. It's probably easy for you to conjure up a picture of happiness, too; you might imagine upright posture and a smiling face.

I'm sure you'll agree that the body language of each mood is vastly different from the other. In other words, each individual state of mind, each specific emotion, involves a particular state of body, or posture.

But there's yet another, less obvious dimension to consider. Your posture; how you hold yourself and move your body, can influence your *mood*.

The next time you get depressed, remember that you don't *have* to stay in a funk (unless you want to, of course). In the future, instead of drooping or slumping as you normally would when depressed, straighten up. Instead of moving slowly, speed up. Instead of frowning, smile! Force yourself to vigorously clap, dance, exercise, or move in an expansive way. Changing your state of body will change your state of mind.

Try this the next time you're feeling down, and you will magically transform your mood from being in a funk to feeling funky!

*Oh, what great heights
we all could reach,
if only we'd practice
what we preach!*

— *C. Leslie Charles*

If I Were You...

The world would be a great place if only other people would take our advice, wouldn't it? How often do you make suggestions to others, offer a bit of wisdom, or tell it like it is? And how seldom do you observe others immediately applying your sage advice?

Sometimes a situation can seem so obvious to us, the outsider. We witness a friend's conflict or dilemma and while the answer may be crystal clear to us, it's anything but clear to the other party. We may secretly marvel that they could be so totally out of touch.

But let's be objective for a moment and turn things around. How often do other people give *you* advice, offer suggestions, or provide counsel?

The point? Maybe we all need to listen more closely to our own advice! For example, have you ever told anyone to lighten up, quit whining, or get off square one? And have you ever needed to hear that very thing? Maybe *we* miss the obvious, too!

Life could be less complicated and troublesome if each of us simply took the advice we so freely give to others. Indeed, the world might be a better place if we were all willing to capitalize on our own wisdom. Maybe you will think about this the next time you begin to say, "If I were you..."

*When we try to
"pay back" other people
we increase our
emotional indebtedness to them.*

— *C. Leslie Charles*

The High Cost Of Paybacks

Bad things happen to all of us and merely wishing them away won't make it so. Recovering from a major loss, hurt, disappointment, or unjust event can be difficult, but when you consider the alternative (depression, anger, blame, stress, heartache), why choose to prolong the misery?

While we may not *knowingly* do so, there are times when we perpetuate a distressing situation. We get stuck in our attempts to blame, seek justice, or make a guilty party suffer. We are unable to grasp that revenge is beyond our jurisdiction.

If you have fallen prey to this mentality, consider that you're letting emotional pain take precedence over moments of joy and closeness with people you love. You're allowing something from the past to infect your present (and possibly your future). Though none of us can live a pain-free existence, we deserve as much inner peace as we can find.

Yes, people will treat you unfairly. Injustices will occur. But as long as you attempt to give someone what *you* think they deserve, your own emotional debt load increases. Resist sacrificing your well-being in the cause of a "justice" that may never be served.

Let it go, come to terms with the situation, and move beyond the pain so you can get on with your life and get more of what *you* deserve—more payoffs, and fewer paybacks.

In the absence of feedback we make up our own version of reality.

— *C. Leslie Charles*

If In Doubt, Check It Out

While we know it is impossible to read someone else's mind, many of us act as if we can. We commonly draw our own conclusions about why people behave as they do rather than checking things out.

We attach our own meanings to the words or actions of others without clarifying or questioning the intent of the other party. We interpret statements or events as holding a particular significance without challenging our logic or verifying our perceptions. What's the possible problem with this?

Second guessing another person's motives can create unnecessary conflict, misunderstandings, hurt feelings, or disappointment. If we fail to discuss the issues in question, we will never know for certain if our interpretation is right or wrong.

Couples sometimes fall into a pattern of erroneous interpretations of a partner's behavior without discussing or questioning what's going on. Workers decide that their boss has a case against them with no evidence other than silence. Friends drift apart because of unverified assumptions each makes about the other. Does this have to happen? No!

The next time there's a question in your mind, ask. With so much at stake, it bears knowing for certain. You'll be further ahead by checking up on things rather than making them up.

*We tend to learn better lessons
from our mistakes
than our successes—
so let's learn to celebrate
our disasters.*

—*C. Leslie Charles*

One Step At A Time

At some point in life, we all face that lonely, unguarded moment of reckoning. Standing in front of a mirror, aghast, unclothed, we scan our overweight, out of shape body, asking, "How did I let myself get this way?" Or we may find ourself in the throes of a self-imposed crisis asking this same regretful question.

Those agonizing moments spent admitting to our short sightedness are among the loneliest in all the world. We ask, "How did I get here?" But we know the answer—one step at a time. A series of decisions, some of them conscious, some of them not, brought us to this moment of realization.

Looking back, events crystallize, and as the pieces fall into place, we sadly realize how we avoided or dismissed those little warning signs and signals as they surfaced along the way.

In moving on, we learn once again that to be alive is to be aware, and choice is best made a conscious activity. We recognize that there is no easy way back; no convenient short cuts. Just as we wound up where we are as the result of a gradual process, we recover from a setback or trauma in the same manner; one step at a time.

Rather than doing ourself the disservice of expecting instant success, healing, or forgiveness, we must be realistic. Rebuilding is best done in the same way we created our situation, through the process of gradualism: one step at a time.

*Make it easy
for people to give you
what you want or need from them.*

— *C. Leslie Charles*

Give Out What You Want Back

Have you ever found yourself taking on the mood of the company you're sharing? This might be okay if you're surrounded by happy, upbeat, positive people, but that's probably not always the case. Perhaps you've succumbed to the foul mood of a cranky family member, grumpy neighbor, or stodgy boss.

How about when you're at the mercy of a surly, indifferent, rude, or uncaring clerk, customer, or co-worker? What do you do?

When faced with someone else's bad mood, do you as a rule, respond in kind? While this is a natural reaction, it unfortunately seals your fate for slipshod treatment. If you truly want to get the respect you deserve, try this: do the exact opposite of what your instincts tell you to do.

Rather than snapping back, be friendly, attentive, responsive, and empathic. It's very likely you will watch that petulant person transform before your eyes! Easy? No! This is not the most "natural" reaction in the world, but it *is* an effective one.

This allows you to maintain control of the interaction, and redefines the conditions under which the two of you will relate.

You'll be amazed at how quickly people come around when you insist on friendly treatment—by first giving it out.

*Every day, make one person smile
who wasn't expecting to.
Maybe that person will be you!*

— *C. Leslie Charles*

Keep Smiling!

We've often heard the phrase, "what's inside shows on the outside;" that our moods show through on our face. Recent research suggests that the opposite is also true: that the look on our *face* can affect our moods.

In one research project, subjects were instructed to change their facial expressions without the use of words such as happy, sad, scared, surprised, and so on. The research participants were asked to raise or lower their eyebrows, squint or open their eyes wide, purse their lips or draw the corners of their mouth to an open, upward, or downward position.

There was never any mention of emotion during the instruction. In other words, subjects simply mimicked the facial movements we commonly associate with emotions such as surprise, happiness, sadness, fear, or anger. They then completed a survey describing their responses to the experience.

Reported emotional reactions tended to match the look that had been created on their faces. Subjects who mirrored negative expressions reported feeling uncomfortable or uneasy during the project, and those who had "smiled" reported their experience as positive.

The point? If you're in a bad mood, smile. If you're feeling down, look like you're feeling up. What shows on the outside can affect the inside. The results are conclusive—keep smiling!

What do you want
to have happen in this situation:
do you want to be right,
or get results?

— *C. Leslie Charles*

When Being Right Might Be Wrong

Sometimes in the midst of a conflict, or as we wade through the aftermath of a miscommunication, our priorities go haywire. We might spend far more time trying to find the culprit than trying to find a solution. Or, rather than attempting to solve a problem, our anger may drive us to search for clever ways of forcing other people into admitting they were wrong.

Think about how much time you've wasted in your life; how much effort you've put into having to "be right" rather than working toward positive results. This is especially pertinent when dealing with someone you love, because you're both on the same team!

In most instances, attempting to resolve the situation would make more sense than wasting time splitting hairs over who was at fault. Begin by clarifying your *intent*. Even if the other party *is* wrong, so what?

In the workplace, at home, or in social situations, please keep in mind; there's a big difference between being right and getting results.

Of course, there may be isolated times when you will choose the satisfaction of "being right," over working toward results, but think things through carefully ahead of time.

When a valued relationship is at stake, stop and ask yourself, "What is my intent, and why?" This will help you focus on the long term rewards of the relationship over the short term "win" of being right.

*In life,
the ultimate control
is letting go.*

— *C. Leslie Charles*

The Issue Of Control

Are you a "control" person? We all grapple with control issues and regardless of what your specific issues may be, here is a general strategy for handling them more effectively.

It may sound crazy, but the most effective application of control is learning how to let go. Let me offer an everyday example: most of us, when driving a car under threatening conditions, tend to hold the steering wheel with tight, tense hands. While this may *seem* to be the best choice, we actually have less control over our car than when we are relaxed. In other words, for greater control, we need to relax and let go.

It's the same way in life, or when dealing with people; if your instincts tell you to tighten up, you need to do the exact opposite—loosen up instead. Let your brain override your instincts.

This is a great rule with universal application in a variety of demanding situations. Smile when you're tempted to scream; take a deep breath before you instinctively react. In general, just relax and loosen up. Remind yourself of this principle the next time you want to force an issue, deliver an ultimatum, or make demands on another person. True control is letting go!

*Learning to live with a loss
helps us gain
in depth of character.*

— *C. Leslie Charles*

When The Going Gets Rough

Despite my optimistic attitude, I'll be the first to admit that life can be rough. There's nothing lonelier than dealing with the heavy, heart wrenching pain of loss, yet at some point each of us will face it.

In 1984 when my youngest son, Rob, was killed in a work accident, I didn't know how or if I would ever recover from the shock, anger, and grief I felt. A neighbor of mine, who had lost two adult children, told me that time helps us heal. It's true.

Maybe right now, while you're reading this book, you are facing a major loss. I wish there was something I could do or say to magically relieve your pain and help you feel better immediately. But I can't.

You can, however, help yourself by initiating a temporary period in which to grieve, be angry, work through your guilt, feel sorry for yourself, or just think (even about morbid things).

As you sort through your feelings, it is important for you to believe that you *will* eventually heal. Time will be your ally and along the way, you will discover some valuable insights you might never have learned otherwise.

Even in losing a loved one we can choose to honor them as we live on by holding a cherished and joyful memory instead of condemning ourself to lifelong grieving and pain.

*Choose to live consciously
and deliberately;
some people cruise through life
on automatic pilot.*

— *C. Leslie Charles*

Switching Channels

When you're driving down the road and a song comes on the radio, if it's one you hate, what do you do? Switch stations? That's a common practice when listening to the radio or watching TV, but how about in life?

Do you exercise the same option when things pop into your mind or do you allow yourself to be victimized by whatever comes along? When negative or undermining thoughts stream into your mind, you don't have to let these insidious thought waves take over. You can switch "mental stations."

Your self-talk patterns affect how you feel and act; the thoughts you create and repeat over and over again shape your self-esteem and emotional well-being. And you can consciously choose the specific program you want to hear. You can literally *select* the thoughts you want to focus on.

I can attest that my self-talk is markedly different today than when my self-esteem was low and I allowed negative thinking patterns to dominate. Things changed drastically once I realized I could reset my "mental dial."

The next time an undermining or negative thought comes into your head, consciously replace it with a positive one. Your ability to switch mental stations guarantees you'll keep your thoughts on the proper wave length. Stay tuned!

How ironic to think we might consider betting on ourself to be a gamble!

— *C. Leslie Charles*

Trust Me

One insight I would hope you'll gain from this book is to acknowledge how much you have going for yourself. I hope you will learn to trust that. You are wiser than you think you are and you know more than you think you know.

For example, you're familiar with many of the ideas presented here. You've thought about them, and applied many of them, but you have also doubted your abilities at times.

Please trust that you have what it takes to enrich your life and make it closer to what you want it to be. You already have, deep inside you, the know-how, logic, wisdom, instincts, and persistence to create a fulfilling life for yourself. Do you believe that?

Many of us don't. Some of us think we somehow have to become a whole new, different person first before we can take charge of our life. But that's not true. All we have to do is be honest about who we are and trust the knowing parts of ourself; to consistently apply our inner wisdom and allow our positive qualities to drive our decisions.

We need to quit second guessing ourself and others. We need to be less driven by obligation, less inclined to make up weak excuses, and more open and direct with others. In short, we need to trust ourselves.

Go ahead, try it. Trust that you will do what's right for you. And trust me, it will work!

*For quality in your life,
either care about what you do
or do what you care about.*

— *C. Leslie Charles*

Feeding Your Spirit

In this age of convenience items and high technology time savers, many of us are feeling more hurried and harried than ever. Each day has its extensive "to-do" list; we rush from one thing to another, and still don't have time to get everything done. It's as if we're too busy to truly live, and if you are nodding your head in agreement, maybe it's time to take stock.

The question is simple: how do your spend your time, and how do you feel about that? If you feel chronically rushed, overwhelmed, buried, or spread too thin, it's time to rediscover the little things you can do (or *not* do) to "up" the level of quality in your life.

Slow down. Reexamine your values. Reclaim your time. Remind yourself of what is truly important. Savor the special touches, activities, and rituals you consider inherently relaxing, renewing, or rewarding.

Commit to adding more quality time in your life, for yourself and those you love. Find, and *do*, the things that "feed your spirit" and help you maintain your perspective. Learn to say "no" and eliminate unnecessary demands, hassles, and stressors that diminish your vitality.

Life is too brief to be lived in a hurry! You deserve to spend more of your time doing the things that feed your spirit, nourish your mind, and bring you joy.

If you're going to put something off, start with procrastination.

— *C. Leslie Charles*

Not To Be Put Off

We may say we are willing to grow and change, but it takes more than intent to do it.

Perhaps you made a recent personal promise to work on a new behavior or evaluate a conflict in your life. But despite your good intentions, your promise lapsed into procrastination. Let's face it; just *knowing* you need to do something is not always enough to propel you into action. It's regrettably easy to put things off and even easier to outright *avoid* them, especially if they are challenging, intimidating, or will temporarily complicate your life.

For example, I put off beginning my first book project for well over a year although it was extremely important to me. I had to overcome my self-doubt and insecurity before I could begin. It took some work but look at the results!

What are you putting off? What personal issues are you choosing to avoid right now? What is lurking in the back of your mind that occasionally resurfaces with an uneasy lurch?

Dr. Harold Bloomfield warns us that "What we resist, persists." Those things you're avoiding often have more staying power than you do. They'll wait and if you're lucky you will get to them sooner or later. But later may be too late! Better to make a choice driven by *desire* rather than regret.

Most of all, consider the rewards of grabbing the bull by the horns before it comes after you!

*It's one thing to list your priorities
and it's quite another
to live by them.*

— *C. Leslie Charles*

Life's "High Five"

If you were asked to list the five things that are absolutely the most important to you in your life, what would they be? Write them down.

Then ask yourself if you are living, on a daily basis, in harmony with those five items. How does your daily behavior reflect your "High Five?"

If, for example, you listed health as being important, what do you do each day to enhance your physical and mental well-being?

If you listed specific relationships and people, what are you doing or saying to them each day that conveys how important they are to you? In other words, are you living in line with your priorities?

Perhaps there is something you've been putting off because you are so busy, or you've been waiting for that perfect moment. How long will you wait? Some of us don't act on our priorities until we are forced to. And sometimes, regrettably, by then it's too late. Perhaps these thoughts can help you identify what's most important to you and help you set (or reset) your priorities.

You know that it's not what we say—but what we *do* that counts. When it comes to major priorities, I hope you are making every single day reflect your "High Five." What higher priority could there be?

TAKE TEN!

A reminder that the little things in life
can make a big difference

10 minutes of _____

—I am the key to my success —

I would like to encourage you to make photocopies of the **TAKE TEN** card shown above. Clip them to size and carry them with you, ready as an instant reminder. Give them to friends, to significant others, to yourself. Use them as an inspiration to get what you need in life—from others and from yourself.

If you would like a couple of "real" **TAKE TEN** cards fresh from our factory, just mail a stamped, self-addressed envelope and I'd be happy to send them along.

Take Ten!

Motivational speakers encourage us to think big and dream big. That's fine for goals, but for everyday life, there's virtue in thinking small, too. For example, we all want to be productive, and we often wait for huge, uninterrupted blocks of time in which to complete our tasks.

Yet it's no surprise that these extended periods of time seldom occur. So instead of waiting for the unlikely, here are a few of the things you can do in only ten minutes at a time:

- read a brief inspirational passage or short article
- organize your office or work area
- clean a drawer or refrigerator shelf
- catch up on your filing or make a quick phone call
- work on your goals: visualize, or repeat positive affirmations
- relax with deep breathing; reduce your stress
- listen to someone you love; give them your complete, total attention
- exercise or stretch

Is ten minutes significant? The ten minute note you send is ten times more valuable than a five page letter that never gets written. If you waste ten minutes a day, at the end of a year you will have lost one full work week! *Invest* that ten minutes instead. Think big, dream big, but start small. When in doubt, take ten.

*Persistent people
don't know they can't do it;
they just keep on trying
until they succeed.*

— *C. Leslie Charles*

STICK TO IT!

If there is something you want; a way of thinking, living, feeling, or being, do what you can to make it happen. You deserve the absolute best life you can create, and it's up to you to give yourself that gift. No one else can do it for you; *it's up to you.*

I hope you'll take the time and energy to identify and explore your dream, and work toward it. Create the image, visualize it in your mind, and hold onto it. Keep thinking about what it will take to make it happen and eventually, you will devise a systematic, step-by-step plan. And, in the course of your journey, I hope you'll cultivate an unshakable belief in your ability to achieve your goal, because you *already* possess the capacity to make it happen.

Remind yourself to be patient so you can work toward what you want in a persistent, day-by-day process. Your determination, self-belief, and persistence will help clear the path. Yes, there will be unknowns, but you can work through them.

You will need to be flexible and resilient, because at times you'll face frustration, fear, and maybe even failure or temporary setbacks.

But you have the ability, and the right, to get back up and start over, anywhere, any time, regardless of the obstacle. As you work toward what you want, stay focused on your goal, believe in yourself, and in spite of it all, *STICK TO IT!*

The Charles Law of Opposites

The Charles Law of Opposites

We all struggle with our own inconsistencies. While we may have a strong sense of what we want, or what's right for us, we often interfere with our attempts to get it. In other words, knowing what we want or need to do doesn't mean we'll do it.

It takes a lot of effort, persistence, and self-understanding to make things happen, yet sometimes we give up rather than use these qualities to push through our fear or resistance. We've all heard the phrase, "You are your own worst enemy."

Sometimes, despite our earnest desire or positive intent, we undermine our efforts. We back up instead of advance, or fail to take action when it is most appropriate. It's as if every time we need to take a step forward, there are forces ready to push us back, or keep us where we are.

I call it the "Law of Opposites" and I think you'll identify. Put simply, the Law of Opposites states that for every positive intent there seems to be equal inertia or resistance preventing us from taking action.

The following examples may give you the inspiration to prevail in future situations that might have gotten the best of you in the past.

With vision, belief, and the power of persistence, you can overcome the Law of Opposites.

*For every situation in which we need
to take action
there will be an equal amount of
inertia or resistance.*

—*C. Leslie Charles*

*When we most need
to take good care of ourselves
we will be our most self-indulgent.*

— *C. Leslie Charles*

When we most need criticism we will be our most defensive.

— *C. Leslie Charles*

When we most need to listen we will be our most distracted.

— *C. Leslie Charles*

*When we most need
to keep our mouth shut
we will be most compelled to sound off.*

—*C. Leslie Charles*

*When we most need
to be self-accepting and self-supporting
we will be our most vicious critic.*

— *C. Leslie Charles*

When we most need to be flexible we will be our most unyielding.

— C. Leslie Charles

*When we are most in need
of support or comfort
we are least likely to ask for it.*

—*C. Leslie Charles*

*The message we most need
to hear
is the one we will most resist.*

— *C. Leslie Charles*

*When we most need
to be cautious
we will be our most reckless.*

— *C. Leslie Charles*

When we most need
love
we will be our most unlovable.

— *C. Leslie Charles*

Prevail over
The Law of Opposites
with
positivism,
persistence,
and patience.

— *C. Leslie Charles*

A Special Gift

If I could give you a special gift, it would be...

Unbridled vitality to sustain your mind, body and spirit...

Humor so you would laugh your way through life...

Happiness so you would live with a joyful heart...

Spiritual depth so you would know and trust yourself...

Nurturing relationships so you would celebrate love...

Adaptability so you would change and grow with ease...

Positive persistence so you would prevail against the odds...

Wisdom so you would make magnificent choices.

Yet none of these are mine to give:

Only you can give such a special gift—to yourself.

—C. Leslie Charles

Perspective

I don't have to
know it all or do it all.

I don't need to
have it all or be it all.

What I do need is
to know who I am,
know what I want,
know what makes me happy
and know how to get my needs met.

If I can do that successfully,
all the rest will fall into place.

—C. Leslie Charles

About the Author...

Leslie Charles is a model of persistence and success yet her compelling story starts on the same sad note as that of many confused teenagers.

Pregnant, she left high school after the tenth grade to marry at the tender age of sixteen. The birth of her third child, born just months after Leslie turned twenty, meant she had achieved her goals in life: get married, have kids.

But there was one thing she didn't have: an education. When her children were still tiny, she returned to high school for a brief period, only to drop out a second time.

Following her divorce, Leslie's prospects were grim. Lacking both an education and work skills, the only full-time employment she could find was a low paying secretarial job. She and her children subsisted at poverty level with little hope for the future.

It was during this difficult period that Leslie had a revelation, one that would change the course of her life. She realized that if things were ever going to change, *she* would have to change!

Affecting this personal transformation required some intense soul searching and inward exploration.

Hearing by chance about a state-funded program that could help her attend college, Leslie studied for, and passed, her G.E.D. She then made an appointment with the Department of Social Services where she applied for public assistance, explaining, "I want to improve my life."

Two years on welfare gave Leslie the opportunity she needed: the means to earn an Associate Degree from the local Community College, a chance to acquire work skills, and time to develop a new attitude toward life. And that was only the beginning!

It took Leslie eight years to finish her B.A. in Communication while working full time and raising her children. She then founded her company, TRAININGWORKS, in 1979 and has since worked with over 300 clients and touched thousands of lives.

Leslie's presentations, and now her writings, educate, motivate, and inspire people to realize their full potential. She is proof that persistence is the number one trait of the achiever, and opportunity is the companion of adversity.

A business consultant, leader, and professional speaker, Leslie custom designs and delivers presentations on change management, customer service, and communication skills for clients throughout North America.

Her unique style combines business experience, formal education, and "street smarts." Practical and personable, the rapport she establishes with her audiences puts her in a special category as a speaker.

In addition to her corporate work, Leslie takes the time to address audiences whose lives parallel her own. Because she's "been there," she brings insight, hope, and a rare credibility to each speaking engagement.

Her motto is, *"You are the key to your success"* and her mission is helping others discover their potential by applying the power of positive persistence. Leslie Charles is available to speak to your organization; you can contact her through Yes! Press.

A Special Invitation From the Author

As a new author, I learned that the process of writing a book such as this is a tremendously personal experience. But then, so is *reading* it! I hope you enjoyed your first reading of **STICK TO IT!** and that you'll return to these pages many times. I feel confident it will continue to serve and inspire you.

In reading this book, you and I have connected in a special way. If these words and ideas have touched you, or if you feel you have personally benefited, please let me know; I'd love to hear from you. It is gratifying to discover how different readers apply my ideas; they have described their experiences of holding an *Alive and Well!* party, making a job change, achieving a goal, establishing a new, healthy habit, resolving an old hurt, or improving a relationship as a result of reading this book. These reports are a motivating force for me.

Readers describe **STICK TO IT!** as a book that spans age, gender, and role, for the messages are both timely and timeless. They purchase it as gifts for family and friends. Many readers have told me they share selected portions with their adolescent children or teenagers, and it is a perfect book for you and your partner or spouse to read and discuss together.

I hope **STICK TO IT!** refreshes your outlook: we can learn so much from our experiences if we have the proper attitude. We especially stand to gain from the difficult times, or the occasions when we must stretch our abilities. Please forgive me if I have made anything sound easy or instantly doable. Every conscious choice we make, every mindful step we take is a significant one, and personal improvement is an ongoing, gradual process. My hope is that as you read this book, it will offer you comfort or insight when and where you need it. And even though I wrote these pieces, be assured that I, too, revisit them often.

And just as there will be more experiences for both of us, there will be more books from me. In 1996 I plan to write a book celebrating the strength and character of the human spirit. It will feature a series of short stories describing the challenges and struggles of everyday people; individuals we would never otherwise hear about or read about, but whose stories deserve to be told.

Once the stories are selected, I will personally interview each individual, exploring the details of their experience. Each person featured in the book will receive, free of charge, five autographed, personally inscribed copies for their own use. If you have such a story, or if you know of someone who has faced a major challenge and prevailed in spite of it all, please send a brief synopsis (a paragraph or two) to my attention at **Yes! Press.**

Readers Praise STICK TO IT!

What an inspiration your book **STICK TO IT!** has been to me. I find that I carry it with me almost every place I go—work, weekends away, home, etc. It has been very helpful in so many ways, at a time in my life when I really needed "words of wisdom."

This is an exciting book—it really addresses a lot of issues! I get new ideas with every reading.

I have enjoyed your book immensely, including the copyright statement—how original!

STICK TO IT! is one of the most inspirational books I've read in a long time.

I began my year with a special regimen based around your book: each day I light a candle, read, and then meditate on my "thought for the day" while getting ready for work. Thank you!

Little did I know what a powerful gift I was giving myself when I bought your book. It is magnificent!

I just opened your book to browse for a few moments and find I'm already on page 17! What great, inspiring ideas and insights on the pesky problems that plague us all every day.

I read your book from cover to cover. It's now in our great room on the coffee table and each of us reads from it when we are feeling a little down. It lightens us up.

Order Form

To order additional autographed copies of **STICK TO IT!**
please send $11.95 per copy plus $3.50 shipping and handling.
Shipping is free on orders of 3 or more books sent to the same address.

Enclosed is my check for _____ made payable to **Yes! Press** for _____copies.

Name_____

Address _____

City_____ State _____ Zip_____

As a special free service, Leslie Charles will include a personalized inscription on gift copies. Simply include the name and a brief description of the recipient with your order.

Yes! Press
PO Box 956
East Lansing, MI 48826

Quantity discounts available, please call 1-800-670-7535.

**Leslie Charles designs and presents keynotes and workshops
for conferences, conventions, and in-house meetings.
If you would like to contact her about a speaking engagement,
please call 1-800-670-7535.**

These ideas have changed many lives.
They can change yours.